VERSE
ADELAIDE CRAPSEY

NEW YORK
1915

PUBLIC DOMAIN POETS

Editor: Dick Whyte   —: No. VI :—   June 2022

ADELAIDE CRAPSEY (1878-1914) was born and raised in Brooklyn, New York, and attended Vassar College, where she served as class poet three years in a row. After graduating Crapsey taught history and literature at Kemper Hall in Wisconsin, and then studied at the School of Archaeology in Rome. Around this time she began writing 'free verse', drawing influence from the French *vers libre*, Japanese hokku and tanka, and the work of Yone Noguchi (among others); and in the early-1910s Crapsey developed an unrhymed 5-line poetic form called the 'cinquain', modeled in part on tanka. Unfortunately, Crapsey's life was plagued with illness, and she died in 1914 at the age of 36. While leaving behind just a single short volume of poems – simply titled *Verse*, and published the year following her death (along with an unfinished book on poetics, *A Study of English Metrics*) – Crapsey's work would go on to influence numerous poets central to the post-1913 'new verse' movements, including Marianne Moore, Lola Ridge, Yvor Winters, and Carl Sandburg (et al.).

Selected poems from *Verse* (The Manas Press, 1915; Alfred A. Knopf, 1922); 'November Night', 'Release', 'Triad', 'Moon Shadows', 'Susanna & the Elders', 'Youth', 'The Guarded Wound', 'Night Winds', 'Amaze', 'The Warning', 'Fate Defied', & 'The Lonely Death', also published in *Others: An Anthology of the New Verse* (Alfred A. Knopf, 1916); 'Dirge', 'Triad', 'Moon-Shadows', 'Susanna & the Elders', 'Night Winds', 'Amaze', & 'The Warning' (*Anthology of Magazine Verse*, 1916; *The Golden Treasury of Magazine Verse*, 1918); 'Dirge' (*The Answering Voice: One Hundred Love Lyrics By Women*, 1917); 'Song', 'Fate Defied', 'The Warning', 'The Lonely Death' (*The Second Book of Modern Verse*, 1919), etc. 'Loneliness' was not included in either edition of *Verse*, first published in the *Vassar Miscellany* (1901). Jean Webster's 'Preface' first published in *Vassar Miscellany* (March 1915), and republished in *Verse* (1922); here, followed by excerpts from William Stanley Braithwaite's 'The Idol Breakers' (*The Poetic Year*, 1916).

Cover: 'River', & A. Affeld – 'Sketch' (*The Vassarian*, 1901). Inside: 'Sun-Dial at Hillside, New York', in Alice Morse Earl – *Sun-Dials & Roses of Yesterday* (MacMillan, 1902); J.W. – 'Street' (*The Vassarian*, 1901); 'Sequoia Tree' (*The Stanford Sequoia*, Jan. 1899), etc.

This collection ©2022. All individual poems, illustrations, and ornaments belong to the 'public domain', unless otherwise noted, and may be freely copied and/or distributed. Some elements of the originals may have been marginally edited, for clarity and consistency.

PUBLIC DOMAIN PRESS
Aotearoa / New Zealand
ISBN: 978-0-473-64924-1 (print) • 978-0-473-64925-8 (kindle)
978-0-473-64926-5 (pdf)

Adelaide Crapsey
Cinquains & Other Verse

Preface

Jean Webster & William Stanley Braithwaite,
first published 1915 & 1916.

Cinquains

A selection of cinquains written 1911-1913,
first published 1915.

Poems

A selection of miscellaneous verse,
written 1901-1914.

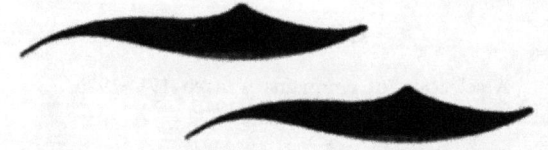

PREFACE

Adelaide Crapsey was, over a term of many years, an eager student of the technical aspects of English poetry. She died on October eighth 1914, after having completed two-thirds of her *Analysis of English Metrics*—an exhaustive scientific thesis relating to accent—which, years before, she had planned to accomplish as her serious life work. Though her mind was intensely preoccupied with the technical and analytical aspects of prosody, still the creative, artistic side of her nature was so spontaneously alive, that she accomplished a very considerable volume of original poetry—almost as a by-product of her study in metrics.

In the gay and somewhat insouciant period of her early days, she could write finished verse with the ease and readiness that the majority of people reserve only for the most commonplace of prose. I have actually known her to produce the book of an acceptable operetta over the week-end! That early work is gone. It lives only in the memory of those who happened to be near her at the time.

She tossed it off as the fleeting expression of a moment, and took no slightest care to preserve it. But several of those early poems stick persistently in my mind over the years, and though I have no copy and cannot quote them accurately, I still believe them worthy of a permanent form. That delightful quality of camaraderie, her quick, bubbling humor she retained to the end in conversation; the sadder, sombre questioning of her inner life attained expression only in the poetry she has left.

These poems, of a gossamer delicacy and finish, are the stronger for the technical knowledge behind them. Likewise, her technical work possessed the more vigor because it was not the result of mere theoretical analysis, but also of the first-hand knowledge gained through her own creative achievement. In each field she spoke with the authority that experience in the other gave. Her studies in prosody were too technical for comprehension by the lay reader. It is through her creative work that she will be remembered, though she herself considered this the slightest part of her accomplishment.

As her study in metrics was astoundingly objective and coldly unreflective of any emotional mood, so her own poems were at the other extreme, astoundingly subjective and descriptive of a mental state that found expression in no other form. They are heart-breakingly sombre; but they are true.

Adelaide Crapsey, by nature as vivid and joyous and alive a spirit as ever loved the beauty of life, like Keats and Stevenson, worked doggedly for many years against the numbing weight of a creeping pitiless disease. In her last year, spent in exile at Saranac Lake, forbidden the strength-sapping work that her metrical study entailed, she was forced to lie and look into space—and these poems grew. Her window looked down upon the Saranac graveyard, "Trudeau's garden," she gaily called it; but its meaning struck home. "To the Dead in the Graveyard Underneath my Window," was among the papers she left behind.

The verse form which she calls "Cinquain" she originated herself. It is an example of extremest compression. She reduces an idea to its very lowest terms—and presents it in a single sharp impression.

In spite of the fact that many of these poems were left only in their first rough draft, they are marvelously perfect. A fastidious distinction marks all of her work—all of her life—it was the most characteristic feature of a very rare nature.

JEAN WEBSTER.

Vassar Miscellany
    March 1915

" The memory of Adelaide Crapsey," Jason continued, " will grow famous like the memory of Emily Dickinson, whom she resembles in the brevity, compact imaginativeness, and mystic glitterings of her art...

" ' Her death was tragic. Full of the desire of life she yet was forced to go, leaving her work all unfinished. Her last year was spent in exile at Saranac Lake. From her window she looked down on the graveyard —" Trudeau's Garden," she called it, with grim-gray irony. Here, forbidden the work her metrical study entailed, these poems grew — flowers of a battlefield of the spirit. But of her passionate revolt against the mandate of her destiny she spared her family and friends even a sign. When they came to cheer and comfort her it was she who brought them cheer and comfort. With magnificent and appalling courage she gave forth to them the humor and gaiety of her unclouded years, saving them even beyond the end from knowledge of this beautiful and terrible testament of a spirit all unreconciled, flashing " unquenched defiance to the stars." ' "

"Yes," he began again, "her poems are the remarkable testament of a spirit 'flashing unquenched defiance to the stars.' The most effective utterance of the poet is in a form invented by Miss Crapsey which she called 'Cinquains.' They are like marvellously chiselled gems. Dynamic in mood or thought, these verses strike upon the reader's attention with surprise and wonderment. This form is undoubtedly a result of work upon which Miss Crapsey was engaged at one time, on the 'Analysis of English Metrics,' and it falls into the scope of the modern movement for new and concentrated expression. The vigor and depth of the poet's emotional and imaginative forces are in these 'Cinquains' at their ripest and fullest. The power to condense an abstract inner mood into this utterance, so concrete, so overpoweringly transformed, has all the evidence of that extraordinary quality we call genius.

What a range of forces is there brought into the compass of a narrow circle. Not a superfluous accessory There is the true quality of mysticism; the keen, cutting imagination slicing through the elementals of existence.

William Stanley Braithwaite
The Idol Breakers (1916)

CINQUAINS
1911-1913

NOVEMBER NIGHT

Listen . . .
With faint dry sound,
Like steps of passing ghosts,
The leaves, frost-crisp'd, break from the trees
And fall.

RELEASE

With swift
Great sweep of her
Magnificent arm my pain
Clanged back the doors that shut my soul
From life.

TRIAD

These be
Three silent things:
The falling snow . . . the hour
Before the dawn . . . the mouth of one
Just dead.

SNOW

Look up . . .
From bleakening hills
Blows down the light, first breath
Of wintry wind . . . look up, and scent
The snow!

ANGUISH

Keep thou
Thy tearless watch
All night but when blue-dawn
Breathes on the silver moon, then weep!
Then weep!

TRAPPED

Well and
If day on day
Follows, and weary year
On year . . . and ever days and years . . .
Well?

MOON-SHADOWS

Still as
On windless nights
The moon-cast shadows are,
So still will be my heart when I
Am dead.

SUSANNA AND THE ELDERS

"Why do
You thus devise
Evil against her?" "For that
She is beautiful, delicate;
Therefore."

YOUTH

But me
They cannot touch,
Old Age and death . . . the strange
And ignominious end of old
Dead folk!

THE GUARDED WOUND

If it
Were lighter touch
Than petal of flower resting
On grass, oh still too heavy it were,
Too heavy!

NIGHT WINDS

The old
Old winds that blew
When chaos was, what do
They tell the clattered trees that I
Should weep?

SHADOW

A-sway,
On red rose,
A golden butterfly . . .
And on my heart a butterfly
Night-wing'd.

AMAZE

I know
Not these my hands
And yet I think there was
A woman like me once had hands
Like these.

THE WARNING

Just now,
Out of the strange
Still dusk . . . as strange, as still . . .
A white moth flew.   Why am I grown
So cold?

MADNESS

Burdock,
Blue aconite,
And thistle and thorn . . . of these,
Singing, I wreathe my pretty wreath
O'death.

FATE DEFIED

As it
Were tissue of silver
I'll wear, O fate, thy grey,
And go mistily radiant, clad
Like the moon.

BLUE HYACINTHS

In your
Curled petals what ghosts
Of blue headlands and seas,
What perfumed immortal breath sighing
Of Greece.

NIAGARA

How frail
Above the bulk
Of crashing water hangs,
Autumnal, evanescent, wan,
The moon.

SAYING OF IL HABOUL

My tent
A vapour that
The wind dispels and but
As dust before the wind am I
Myself.

POEMS
1901–1914

LONELINESS

The earth's all wrapped in gray shroud-
    mist,
  Dull gray are sea and sky,
And where the water laps the land
  On gray sand-dunes stand I.
Oh, if God there be, his face from me
  The rolling gray mists hide;
And if God there be, his voice from me
  Is kept by the moan of the tide.

BIRTH-MOMENT

Behold her,
Running through the waves,
Eager to reach the land:
The water laps her,
Sun and wind are on her,
Healthy, brine-drenched and young,
Behold Desire new-born;—
Desire on first fulfilment's radiant edge,
Love at miraculous moment of emergence,
This is she,
Who running,
Hastens, hastens to the land.

Look . . . Look . . .
Her brown gold hair and lucent eyes of youth,
Her body rose and ivory in the sun . . . .
Look,
How she hastens,
Running, running to the land.

    Her hands are yearning and her feet are swift
    To reach and hold
    She knows not what,
    Yet knows that it is life;
    Need urges her,
    Self, uncomprehended but most deep divined,
    Unwilled but all-compelling, drives her on.
    Life runs to life.

She who longs,
But hath not yet accepted or bestowed,
All virginal dear and bright,
Runs, runs to reach the land.

And she who runs shall be
Married to blue of summer skies at noon,
Companion to green fields,
Held bride of subtle fragrance and of all sweet
    sound,
Belovéd of the stars,
And wanton mistress to the veering winds.

Oh, breathless space between:
Womb-time just passed,
Dark-hidden, chaotic-formative, unpersonal,
And individual life of fresh-created force
Not yet begun:
One moment more
Before desire shall meet desire
And new creation start:
Oh breathless space,
While she,
Just risen from the waves,
Runs, runs to reach the land.

(Ah, keenest personal moment
When mouth unkissed turns eager-slow and
    tremulous
Towards lover's mouth,
That tremulous and eager-slow
Droops down to it:
But breathless space of breath or two
Lies in between
Before the mouth upturned and mouth
    down-drooped
Shall meet and make the kiss.)

Look . . . Look . . .
She runs . . .
Love fresh-emerged,
Desire new-born . . .

        Blown on by wind,
        And shone on by the sun,
        She rises from the waves
        And running,
        Hastens, hastens to the land.

Belovéd and Belovéd and Belovéd,
Even so right
And beautiful and undenied
Is my desire;
Even so longing-swift
I run to your receiving arms.

O Aphrodite!
O Aphrodite, hear!
Hear my wrung cry flame upward poignant-
    glad. . . .
This is my time for me.

I too am young;
I too am all of love!

THE MOTHER EXULTANT
(excerpts)

Joy! Joy! Joy!
The hills are glad,
The valleys re-echo with merriment,
In my heart is the sound of laughter,
And my feet dance to the time of it . . .

Joy! Joy! Joy!
Now is the vision fulfilled:
I have conceived,
I have carried in my womb,
I have brought forth
The life of the world . . .

Joy! Joy! Joy!
Now is the wonder accomplished;
Out of the heart of the living grape
Hath the hand of my belovéd
Wrung the wine of the dream of life.

THE SUN-DIAL

Every day,
Every day,
Tell the hours
By their shadows,
By their shadows.

OLD LOVE

More dim than waning moon
Thy face, more faint
Than is the falling wind
Thy voice, yet do
Thine eyes most strangely glow,
Thou ghost . . . thou ghost.

GRAIN FIELD

Scarlet the poppies
Blue the corn-flowers,
Golden the wheat.
Gold for The Eternal:
Blue for Our Lady:
Red for the five
Wounds of her Son

DIRGE

Never the nightingale,
Oh, my dear,
Never again the lark
Thou wilt hear;
Though dusk and the morning still
Tap at thy window-sill,
Though ever love call and call
Thou wilt not hear at all,
My dear, my dear.

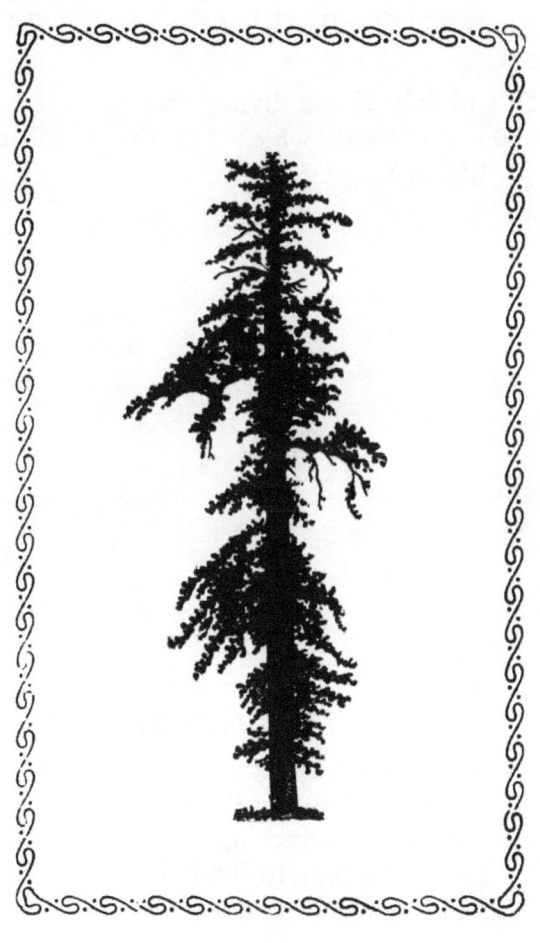

ON SEEING WEATHER-BEATEN TREES

Is it as plainly in our living shown,
By slant and twist, which way the wind hath
    blown?

ADVENTURE

Sun and wind and beat of sea,
Great lands stretching endlessly. . . .
Where be bonds to bind the free?
All the world was made for me!

OH, LADY, LET THE SAD TEARS FALL

Oh, Lady, let the sad tears fall
   To speak thy pain,
Gently as through the silver dusk
   The silver rain.

Oh, let thy bosom breathe its grief
   In such a soft sigh
As hath the wind in gardens where
   Pale roses die.

SONG

I make my shroud but no one knows,
So shimmering fine it is and fair,
With stitches set in even rows.
I make my shroud but no one knows.

In door-way where the lilac blows,
Humming a little wandering air,
I make my shroud and no one knows,
So shimmering fine it is and fair.

VENDOR'S SONG

My songs to sell, good sir!
    I pray you buy.
Here's one will win a lady's tears,
    Here's one will make her gay,
Here's one will charm your true love true
    Forever and a day;
Good sir, I pray you buy!

Oh, no, he will not buy.

My songs to sell, sweet maid!
    I pray you buy.
This one will teach you Lilith's lore,
    And this what Helen knew,
And this will keep your gold hair gold,
    And this your blue eyes blue;
Sweet maid, I pray you buy!

Oh, no, she will not buy.

If I'd as much money as I could tell,
I never would cry my songs to sell,
I never would cry my songs to sell.

THE MOURNER

I have no heart for noon-tide and the sun,
But I will take me where more tender night
Shakes, fold on fold, her dewy darkness down,
And shelters me that I may weep in peace,
And feel no pitying eyes, and hear no voice
Attempt my grief in comfort's alien tongue.

Where cypresses, more black than night is black,
Border straight paths, or where, on hillside
    slopes,
The dim grey glimmer of the olive trees
Lies like a breath, a ghost, upon the dark,
There will I wander when the nightingale
Ceases, and even the veiled stars withdraw
Their tremulous light, there find myself at rest,
A silence and a shadow in the gloom.

But all the dead of all the world shall know
The pacing of my sable-sandal'd feet,
And know my tear-drenched veil along the grass,
And think them less forsaken in their graves,
Saying: There's one remembers, one still
    mourns;
For the forgotten dead are dead indeed.

TO THE DEAD IN THE GRAVEYARD UNDERNEATH MY WINDOW

Written in a Moment of Exasperation

How can you lie so still?   All day I watch
And never a blade of all the green sod moves
To show where restlessly you turn and toss,
Or fling a desperate arm or draw up knees,
Stiffened and aching from their long disuse;
I watch all night and not one ghost comes forth
To take its freedom of the midnight hour.
Oh, have you no rebellion in your bones?
The very worms must scorn you where you lie,
A pallid, mouldering, asquiescent folk,
Meek habitants of unresented graves.
Why are you there in your straight row on row
Where I must ever see you from my bed
That in your mere dumb presence iterate
The text so weary in my ears: "Lie still
And rest; be patient and lie still and rest."
I'll not be patient!   I will not lie still!
There is a brown road runs between the pines,
And further on the purple woodlands lie,
And still beyond blue mountains lift and loom;
And I would walk the road and I would be
Deep in the wooded shade and I would reach
The windy mountain tops that touch the clouds.

My eyes may follow but my feet are held.
Recumbent as you others must I too
Submit?   Be mimic of your movelessness
With pillow and counterpane for stone and sod?
And if the many sayings of the wise
Teach of submission I will not submit
But with a spirit all unreconciled
Flash an unquenched defiance to the stars.
Better it is to walk, to run, to dance,
Better it is to laugh and leap and sing,
To know the open skies of dawn and night,
To move untrammeled down the flaming noon,
And I will clamour it through weary days
Keeping the edge of deprivation sharp,
Nor with the pliant speaking of my lips
Of resignation, sister to defeat.
I'll not be patient.   I will not lie still.

And in ironic quietude who is
The despot of our days and lord of dust
Needs but, scarce heeding, wait to drop
Grim casual comment on rebellion's end;
"Yes, yes. . . . *Wilful and petulant but now
As dead and quiet as the others are.*"
And this each body and ghost of you hath heard
That in your graves do therefore lie so still.

Saranac Lake, N. Y. 1914.

CHIMES

I

The rose new-opening saith,
And the dew of the morning saith,
(Fallen leaves and vanished dew)
Remember death.
    Ding dong bell
    Ding dong bell

II

May-moon thin and young
    In the sky,
Ere you wax and wane
    I shall die:
So my faltering breath,
So my tired heart saith,
That foretell me death.
    Ding-dong
      Ding-dong
        Ding-dong ding-dong bell

III

"Thy gold hair likes me well
    And thy blue eyes," he saith,
Who chooses where he will
    And none may hinder—Death.

At head and feet for candles
    Roses burning red,
The valley lilies tolling
    For the early dead:
Ding-dong ding-dong
Ding-dong ding-dong
Ding-dong ding-dong bell
    Ding dong bell

THE LONELY DEATH

In the cold I will rise, I will bathe
In waters of ice; myself
Will shiver, and shrive myself,
Alone in the dawn, and anoint
Forehead and feet and hands;
I will shutter the windows from light,
I will place in their sockets the four
Tall candles and set them a-flame
In the grey of the dawn; and myself
Will lay myself straight in my bed,
And draw the sheet under my chin.

MY BIRDS THAT FLY NO LONGER

Have ye forgot, sweet birds,
   How near the heavens lie?
Drooping, sick-pinion'd, oh
   Have ye forgot the sky?

The air that once I knew
   Whispered celestial things;
I weep who hear no more
   Upward and rushing wings.

TO MAN WHO GOES SEEKING IMMORTALITY, BIDDING HIM LOOK NEARER HOME

Too far afield thy search.
   Nay, turn. Nay, turn.
  At thine own elbow potent Memory stands,
Thy double, and eternity is cupped
  In the pale hollow of those ghostly hands.

AH ME. . . . ALAS. . . .

(*He*)

Ah me, my love's heart,
Like some frail flower, apart,
High, on the cliff's edge growing,
Touched by unhindered sun to sweeter showing,
Swung by each faint wind's faintest blowing,
But so, on the cliff's edge growing,
From man's reach aloof, apart:
Ah me, my love's heart!

(*She*)

Alack, alas, my lover,
As one who would discover
At world's end his path,
Nor knows at all what faëry way he hath
Who turneth dreaming into faith
And followeth that near path
His own heart dareth to discover:
Alack, alas, my lover!

LO, ALL THE WAY

Lo, all the way,
Look you, I said, the clouds will break, the sky
   Grow clear, the road
Be easier for my travelling, the fields,
   So sodden and dead,
Will shimmer with new green and starry bloom,
   And there will be,
There will be then, with all serene and fair,
   Some little while
For some light laughter in the sun; and lo,
   The journey's end,—
Grey road, grey fields, wind and a bitter rain.

THE WITCH

When I was a girl by Nilus stream
I watched the desert stars arise;
My lover, he who dreamed the Sphinx,
   Learned all his dreaming from my eyes.

I bore in Greece a burning name,
And I have been in Italy
Madonna to a painter-lad,
And mistress to a Medici.

And have you heard (and I have heard)
Of puzzled men with decorous mien,
Who judged—The wench knows far too much—
And hanged her on the Salem green?

AUTUMN

Fugitive, wistful,
Pausing at edge of her going,
Autumn the maiden turns,
Leans to the earth with ineffable
Gesture. Ah, more than
Spring's skies her skies shine
Tender, and frailer
Bloom than plum-bloom or almond
Lies on her hillsides, her fields
Misted, faint-flushing.

                                              Ah, lovelier

    Is her refusal than
    Yielding, who pauses with grave
    Backward smiling, with light
    Unforgettable touch of
    Fingers withdrawn. . . Pauses, lo
    Vanishes . . . fugitive, wistful. . . .

AVIS

"Belle Aliz matin leva."

Avis, the fair, at dawn
Rose lightly from her bed,
Herself arrayed.
Avis, the fair, the maid,
In vestiment of lawn;
Across the fields she sped,
Five flowerets there she found,
In fragrant garland wound,
Avis, the fair, at dawn,
Five roses red.

Go thou from thence of thy pity!
Thou lovest not me.

NIGHT

I have minded me
Of the noon-day brightness,
And the crickets' drowsy
Singing in the sunshine. . . .

I have minded me
Of the slim marsh-grasses
That the winds at twilight,
Dying, scarcely ripple. . . .

And I cannot sleep.

I have minded me
Of a lily-pond,
Where the waters sway
All the moonlit leaves
And the curled long stems. . . .

And I cannot sleep.

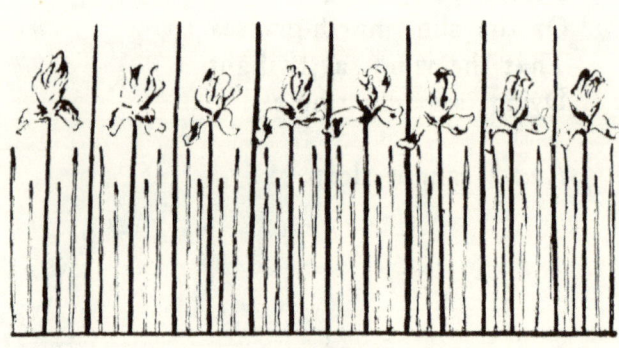

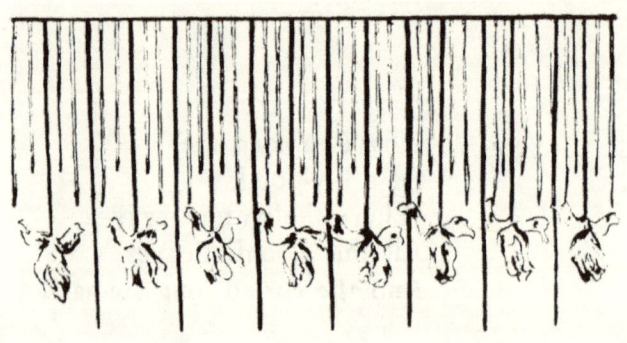

THE IMMORTAL RESIDUE

Wouldst thou find my ashes? Look
In the pages of my book;
And, as these thy hand doth turn,
Know here is my funeral urn.

This Space for Your Thoughts

PUBLICDOMAINPOETS.COM

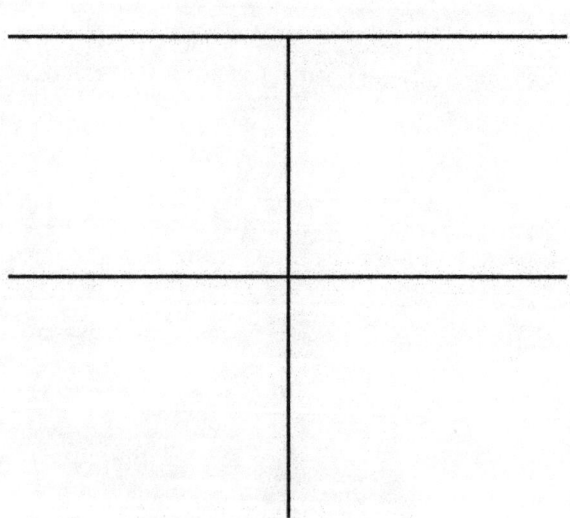

Please handle with care.

www.ingramcontent.com/pod-product-compliance
Lightning Source LLC
Chambersburg PA
CBHW022124040426
42450CB00006B/835